Q[ueen of Peace Media]
books, videos, blogs, prayer
requests, and more, that help you
nurture your faith and

## *Find your way Home.*

**At www.QueenofPeaceMedia.com**
sign up for our newsletter to receive new content.

You can browse through
**Queen of Peace Media's YouTube channel for
help in safely navigating our tumultuous times.**

To be notified of our new YouTube videos,
see www.youtube.com/c/queenofpeacemedia
or go to YouTube.com and search for Queen of
Peace Media, then click "Subscribe" and the
bell icon (top right of the screen).

**Visit Us on Social Media. Like & Follow us!**
Facebook: www.facebook.com/QueenofPeaceMedia
Instagram: www.instagram.com/QueenofPeaceMedia
Pinterest: www.pinterest.com/catholicvideos

# About the author

Christine Watkins (www.ChristineWatkins.com) is an inspirational Catholic speaker and author. Her books include  the highly acclaimed #1 Amazon best-sellers: *The Warning: Testimonies and Prophecies of the Illumination of Conscience (El Aviso: Testimonios y Profecías sobre la Iluminación de Conciencia)*; *Of Men and Mary: How Six Men Won the Greatest Battle of Their Lives (Hombres Junto a María: Así Vencieron Seis Hombres la Batalla Más Ardua de Sus Vidas)*; *Transfigured: Patricia Sandoval's Story (Transfigurada: La Historia de Patricia Sandoval)*. Watkins also authored the Catholic best-seller, *Full of Grace: Miraculous Stories of Healing and Conversion through Mary's Intercession*. Her most recent works are *She Who Shows the Way: Heaven's Messages for Our Turbulent Times*; *Winning the Battle for Your Soul: Jesus' Teachings through Marino Restrepo, a St. Paul for Our Century*; and the upcoming, if not already here, *Marie Julie Jahenny: Prophecies and Protection for the End Times*.

In addition, Watkins has reintroduced an ancient and powerful Marian Consecration to the world, also a #1 best-seller, which is resulting in extraordinary graces for the parishes and people who go through it: *Mary's Mantle Consecration: A Spiritual Retreat for Heaven's Help*, with the accompanying *Mary's Mantle Consecration Prayer Journal (El Manto de María: Una Consagración Mariana para Obtener Ayuda Celestial* y *El Manto de María: Diario de Oración para la Consagración)*. For details, see the end of this book.

Formerly an anti-Christian atheist living a life of sin, Watkins began a life of service to the Catholic Church after a miraculous healing from Jesus through Mary, which saved her from death. Her story can be found in the book, *Full of Grace*. Before her conversion, Watkins danced professionally with the San Francisco Ballet Company. Today, she has twenty years of experience as a keynote speaker, retreat leader, spiritual director, and counselor—with ten years working as a hospice grief counselor and another ten as a post-abortion healing director. Mrs. Watkins lives in Sacramento, California with her husband and three sons.

# IN LOVE
## *with* TRUE
# LOVE

*The unforgettable
story of Sister Nicolina*

**CHRISTINE WATKINS**

©2020 Queen of Peace Media
All rights reserved.
www.queenofpeacemedia.com
Sacramento, California

Unless otherwise indicated, the Scripture texts used in this work are taken from *The New American Bible, Revised Edition (NABRE)* ©2011 by the Confraternity of Christian Doctrine, Washington, DC.

Although every precaution has been taken to verify the accuracy of the information contained herein, the authors and publisher assume no responsibility for any errors or omissions. No liability is assumed for damages that may result from the use of information contained within.

Books may be purchased in quantity by contacting the publisher directly at orders@queenofpeacemedia.com.

ISBN: 978-1-947701-14-4

# Table of Contents

1) ALFRED AND MARIA.................................................11

2) PEDDLING BEHIND ME ...........................................19

3) GRADUATION NIGHT .............................................23

4) LOCKED IN DARKNESS ...........................................27

5) NOT THE NUNNY TYPE ...........................................33

6) LOOKING OUT FOR ME ..........................................39

NOTES TO THE READER ............................................45

OTHER BOOKS BY THE AUTHOR ................................46

# Acknowledgments

This little book is dedicated to Sr. Nicolina Kohler, who made me feel more loved in one hour than many experience in a lifetime. Her radiant smile and nimble way of dispelling my worries with a giggle will forever remind me that life is somehow both crushingly serious and to be taken lightly.

# Introduction

hen I met Sr. Nicolina, the first thing I noticed about her was a lively twinkle. It sparkled in her eyes, her cheeks, and her smile. She was my spiritual director for a time—a period I wished would never end.

That was several years ago, and I wasn't yet a writer, something I never aspired to be. Even after eight books, I still have no desire to be a writer; but as Woody Allen said, "If you want to make God laugh, tell Him your plans." What I did have, and still do, is a passion for sharing information and stories that I believe will help heal the human heart.

One day, as I sat and listened to Sr. Nicolina share gems from her treasure chest of wisdom, she allowed me a glimpse into her past. Intrigued, I wanted to know more. . . and more. . . and couldn't help but think that her engrossing stories should have an audience of much more than one. Sr. Nicolina kindly acquiesced to my request of bringing a recording device to our next spiritual direction appointment— something out of character for her, as she was a private soul. But she decided to trust. . . Three sessions later, I had captured the material for the riveting tale in this book, as well as the edifying story of her experience of a sudden illumination of conscience, as told in the #1 best-selling book, *The Warning: Testimonies and Prophecies of the Illumination of Conscience.*

Most people, I have found, appear to be endlessly restless and dissatisfied, searching for deep meaning and profound love. But finding neither, they pass through life in silent, or not-so-quiet despair. Few are those who seem to have found what all the others are looking for. Sr. Nicolina is one of those few. As I can attest, even after a long day of scrubbing away mold from every surface in a flooded basement, and enduring throbbing knee pain, she still twinkled.

This book is a privileged view into not only a charming soul and an enthralling love story, but into the secrets of Love itself. If you are curious to know the source of Sr. Nicolina's twinkle, continue reading, because the treasure she found is free, and it can be yours, too.

# 1) Alfred and Maria

----------------------------------------

**M**y parents' lives were the greatest love story ever told. Their paths first intertwined when my twenty-three-year-old father spied my eighteen-year-old mother from afar and wiggled his way into the reception room of her all-girls' convent school. His extroverted charm won her over, and conversation flowed. My father loved my mom from that moment forward.

My mom soon loved him, too, and in time became a stay-at-home wife, raising four girls and three boys, while my father became an upstanding leader in agriculture, working in our small town of Oberschwappach, Germany. My parents' devotion to each other and to God never wavered, while their discipline in the home never outshined their playfulness. On weekends our kitchen turned into a miniature family dance hall, with my dad extending his arm to twirl and spin my mom, and with us kids, seated along the wall, ready to jump up and take our turn at the foxtrot or swing. At night, we often heard our folks chatting in the bedroom. Dad would often erupt into laughter, followed by his smoker's cough, over something my quiet, dry-humored mom must have said about one of us.

The only heated words we seven children ever heard between them were, "Let's talk about that tonight." Disagreements stayed in the bedroom. My father never called my mother names. He never shouted at her. He never acknowledged when one of her meals emerged from the oven sub-perfect, and he never left the table without a gracious, "Thank you." My brothers, who became exemplary men and husbands in their own right heard repeatedly from their dad, "You can never deal unkindly with women. If you treat them poorly, you will not keep them for yourself. They will run home." Banter between my parents was never rude or flippant, but conscious and from the heart. Their relationship had no empty words.

In their last few days on earth, my ninety-year-old father, with late stage kidney disease, lay in a twin bed adjacent to my eighty-nine-year-old mother, suffering from heart disease and diabetes. Unbeknownst to them, I casually peeked through a half-opened door one evening, and through that crack, entered into the private intimacy of their hearts. My elderly and frail father got out of his bed, walked over to his wife, leaned over her, and with the greatest of care, placed his trembling hand gently on her cheek, and said, "You're as beautiful to me right now as on the day I met you." Then she reached up to touch his hand and whispered softly, "You will always be my man."

No human love, I felt, could compare to that of my parents'—Alfred and Maria. Not only did their love color my hopes but painted my future, which uncannily dovetailed into their past. The name my parents gave me is Maria, and at age eighteen, I started dating a twenty-three year old named Alfred. From age fourteen on, I worked in a parish ministering to girls who were two years younger than I, and Alfred oversaw the youth ministry for boys in eight parishes. Because he came my way quite often when we did group activities, I came to know his naturally honest and straightforward manner, and he my trenchant, slippery, and roundabout nature. Immediately, I could see that there was something different about him. Athletic and strong, yet gentle as a lamb, with dark hair and dancing eyes, he sported his heart on his sleeve.

Alfred was a true, modern-day cavalier. When driving by my house, he would drop off flowers, freshly picked from the field, leaving them on my bedroom window sill. When I walked toward a car, he opened the door to the passenger seat. At parties, he held out his hand for a dance. I found his charm as embarrassing as it was appealing. Gifted in playing the saxophone, the clarinet, the drums, and guitar, he'd strum and sing my name in romantic fun, and the more times I told him to stop, the more ways he figured out how to sing it, and sing it louder.

Not every German man was like this. I had other short-term boyfriends, but they rushed too quickly into personal sensual indulgence, which I didn't like, and the relationships never lasted. With Alfred, everything was different than what I'd known. Together we shared a common faith, worked as Catholic youth leaders, and held a zealous anti-war stance, as did all the Catholic youth after World War II. Together we hiked, mounted horses, took long bicycle rides, and held hands. But there was something inside of Alfred that we didn't share. At times, Alfred left my side to go to church and told me he was going to sit in front of the Blessed Sacrament. Just sit there by himself? I questioned. When Mass isn't happening? Alfred? The popular, fun-loving youth minister, who played all sorts of instruments and sports and got involved in anything and everything? I didn't believe it.

One summer afternoon when we started dating, Alfred stopped by where I was working at a doctor's office as a receptionist, to discuss what we were doing over the weekend, and then he left. It was twilight, and he said he was going to Ritterkapelle Church. I felt suspicious.

When the clinic closed, I bicycled to the church, parked my bike, and peeked through the vestibule doors into the sanctuary. I saw no one. Darkness had already blanketed the inside, for the sun sets suddenly in Germany. Slowly and silently, I opened the doors into the sanctuary, tiptoed inside, and sat down in the back pew. "Ha! I knew it!" I thought, staring into a dark, empty sanctuary. "He is not going to church."

Then as my eyes adjusted to the darkness, I noticed a figure in the front pew, sitting hauntingly still. As forms took shape in my vision, and I soon made out a human frame. I couldn't believe it. What in the world was Alfred doing in a dark church, quiet like a mouse? I waited . . . and waited. Naturally, time felt long to me, because I didn't want to be discovered. I wasn't accustomed to silent prayer, and he just sat there . . . motionless. *"What is he doing?"* After a few nervous minutes, I slipped out of the church and returned to the office for night duty.

The following weekend, I asked him, "Alfred, what are you doing when you go to church, and there is nothing happening there?"

He looked at me with a suspicious expression, as if to say, "I don't want to tell you, because I don't trust you not to make fun of something so special and personal." When it came to pious matters, I could be flippantly irreverent, calling nuns "walking chapels" and "traffic obstacles," and labeling pious people "religious nutcakes." Fearing I'd say yes, Alfred asked hesitantly, "Well, do you really want to know?"

"It's just that I know there's nothing going on in the

church, and I would never go to a church if nothing was happening there."

"Okay, well," he responded. "I love to be in the church by myself." And that ended that conversation. He'd offer only small slices of his internal pie; but I didn't stop bringing it up because private interior life intrigued and eluded me.

Alfred didn't trust me. He knew if he shared his prayer life with me, I would have no idea what he was talking about. My questions gave away the fact that, even though I'd been a youth minister for many years, I had no experience talking to God.

Finally, one evening, when we were reading a romance together and discussing it with one another, I said to him, "I'm not interested in that book. What I'd really like to know is how to talk to God."

He looked up at me and could tell I was serious. Taking a deep breath, he put the book down. Then he looked at me with great wariness mixed with a twinge of hope. "Are you sure you want to know?"

I nodded, "Yes."

"Well, I guess I should go back in time a bit to explain. . ." Alfred then shared with me pieces from his past I knew little about. "When I was ten, my father was drafted into the war and captured by the Russians. He was put in prison for eight years. The Russians said there weren't any prisoners left on their soil, so my mom and I thought we'd never see my father again. When I turned fourteen, I asked my mom if I could enter the Salesian home for boys who were discerning the priesthood, and she thought it was a good idea since I didn't have a father around. I was in the seminary for four years until Konrad Adenauer (the chancellor of West Germany) went into Russia in 1952 and brought the last prisoners out of

Siberia. It's a miracle that Dad was found alive. When he came home, he took me out of seminary—probably because I am his only kid—and brought me back home.

"So, when I was in the minor seminary, the Salesian priests sometimes brought us into the sanctuary and led us into prayer. One of the things they taught us was a certain kind of meditative prayer, and I loved it. We would sit in front of the Blessed Sacrament, and through this meditative prayer, I could bring my father into my heart and rest with him there, in the full presence of Jesus."

"Can you teach me how to do that?" I asked.

"If you want. But I've never told anybody, and I will teach you, only if you promise not to laugh and never tell anyone about it."

After I promised, Alfred began to lead me into prayer: "Close your eyes. Become very still. Call on Jesus. Repeat His Name, like you might repeat my name, over and over, until it becomes very sweet to your heart. And then when you can feel it, not only think it, then hold it. Stay with Jesus and allow your spirit to get quiet. Taste Him and hold him, and let yourself be held. Then let go of repeating His Name. If you desire to, put your head to Jesus' breast and hear His heart beat, but don't talk. Remain very still, and just be, in the silence."

He paused, deep in thought, and then continued: "I like to pray in the twilight because everything else disappears, and I can focus more easily on God. I also like to bring others into communion with me, into His love. When you come to mind, I ask Jesus to look after you, and by me bringing you there, you enter into a triune relationship with us. That's why I feel very at home when I am with you. I already have you at home with me in prayer."

At first, I could only pray in stillness and silence when Alfred accompanied me. But slowly, as I spent time practicing alone, bringing all that was in my heart before Jesus, I began to experience myself melting into communion with Him. Soon I looked forward to my times of prayer, which now felt so peaceful, centering, and personal. No longer could I throw barbs and sarcasms Alfred's way, when it came to religious matters because I could tell that he was not religious from outside in, like I was. He was religious from the inside out.

IN LOVE WITH TRUE LOVE

# 2) Peddling behind me

Alfred and I grew much closer after I began to truly communicate with God, and in time, we became inseparable. Our relationship had come a long way, and his virtue had rubbed off on me, even before we were a couple. Our first big fight happened when he was twenty and I sixteen, just when I was starting to enjoy his presence. At a monthly meeting of youth ministry leaders, I announced that I had dismissed a girl named Hanelore from my Catholic youth group because I'd already warned her two times not to break the group rules by sleeping around with boys, and she had done it again.

Alfred raised his hand and said to the moderator of the group leaders, "Don't you think there could be a way to hold the weak in our friendship, rather than kick them out? I believe this is exactly what we exist for. Maybe what she needs is friendship."

As soon as the gathering ended, I shot out of the meeting on my bicycle. How dare he contradict and humiliate me! He didn't have to say that crazy idea in front of 120 other people!

After three kilometers, I heard someone peddling behind me, gaining ground. "Oh no, it's him." I started to bike furiously. Sure enough, Alfred passed me on the right. Then he turned his bike sideways and blocked me: "We have to talk."

"I have nothing to say. Let me go home," I blurted, out of breath.

"Well, I cannot stop you here on the street. It wouldn't be a good sight. Can I bicycle home with you and see why you are so upset?"

"Go home."

"Wow," he responded, taken aback. "What did I say?"

Too angry to answer, I hopped on my bike and rattled along past him, but eventually ran out of steam and had to dismount.

"If you're walking, I'm walking, too." I didn't like him doing that either. People we knew were walking by, and I didn't want to be seen with him. "You won't get rid of me, just let your anger out. I really mean well. If it had been someone else, I wouldn't have challenged that person; but because it was you, I wanted to speak since I think you could have done better."

"Well, why did you have to do that in front of people?" I snapped.

"Ah ha! That's what it is!" he exclaimed. "It's your stupid pride. We are there in that meeting to learn. That's the whole purpose. Maybe I should explain a little better why I said what I did and what I think might happen to that girl now that you kicked her out. Her life could get worse without her having a good place to go. I believe her father drinks, and her home life probably isn't good. Have you noticed she never wants to go home? And now she doesn't have the youth group, either. She doesn't have to be your intimate friend, but help her to be part of your circle. Invite her to activities. It would be one way to try to get her away from her bad habits."

As Alfred continued to share his ideas, I softened a bit.

Before riding away, he said, "You think about it and let me know if there could be another way."

Alfred never waited for my answer. He brought Hanelore back in and simply said to the leaders, "I met Hanelore in town. What about taking her back into your group? She'll really give it a good try this time. Right, Hanelore?" Wide-eyed Hanelore nodded yes. That day, the group welcomed her back into the youth group, due to Alfred's initiative, and Hanelore changed. A few years later, she married a good man.

Hanelore wasn't the only female Alfred readied for marriage. He never stopped challenging the flaws in my spirited, flirtatious, and irreverent nature, while at the same time, loving me for who I was. From the moment Alfred and I began dating, marriage entered our thoughts, and God joined our conversations. We loved spending time together—it didn't matter what we were doing, and I became the center of Alfred's life. He always had much more fire in his heart than I. It burned in his eyes. But his high moral standards always kept him controlled, and there was never sex between us. Cherishing God's command and the romantic ideal that we would give ourselves to each other on our wedding night, we supported one another in this goal.

When I was nineteen going on twenty, and Alfred had just turned twenty-four, he received his master's in metal arts, the same trade as his father. Just after his coming graduation, we would have to endure a long-distance relationship. He would be leaving for the Alps to be a summer camp counselor and then work for a year at jobs in metal work, which he had lined up in southern Germany. But I still had two more years of college to go.

# IN LOVE WITH TRUE LOVE

# 3) Graduation night

────────────────────────────────

The first of May, 1956, was Alfred's graduation. That night in northern Germany was bright, warm, and starlit. It couldn't have been more perfect. Alfred had managed to borrow the station wagon from his father's business, even though few cars were left, due to the commandeering of World War II. He walked up to my door in a dapper suit of his favorite dark-blue, topped with a black bow tie. I received him in a turquoise dress that covered my neck with a tightly closed white collar and spread downward from the bodice into turquoise tiers. As always, he exclaimed, "You look beautiful tonight."

Rolling along in the station wagon, we pulled up excitedly to Alfred's school hall in the nearby small town of Hassfurt. The graduation celebration was already in full force with dance music from his own band vibrating in the air. Alfred got out of the car, walked around to my side, opened my door, held out his hand ceremoniously, and we entered the hall arm in arm—into an evening of waltzes, tangos, and lively sambas.

In Alfred's small school, with only about five students in a year's class, each graduate was invited to do a dance with the song and partner of his choice. When Alfred's turn came, he escorted me onto the dance floor, while everyone stood up and clapped. Soon I was lifted across the floor, dancing the waltz with the most romantic man in Germany. Our love filled the room, with sparks flying onto those around us. I wasn't just dancing. My body felt as though it was being swirled into heaven by a human angel.

We stopped as the music ended, just alongside our youth chaplain, Father Hafe, who called out to us joyfully, "If you marry, you'd better ask me to bless your wedding!"

When the celebration ended, a group of friends saw us off with a trail of laughter and shouts of goodwill. As we pulled away in the station wagon, I thought it strange that no one came with us, since normally our friends would pile in the back to elongate the festivities. We were together and alone. Suddenly, a strange feeling came over me, and I couldn't explain it. Finally, we were alone, and normally such a moment would make me very happy. But I felt the opposite. As we continued on, I noticed that Alfred wasn't driving us home, but into his father's forest.

During World War II, when Alfred's father was a prisoner of war, he made a vow with God that if he ever came home, he would build a little chapel to Mary. He remained good to his promise, and now, among a cluster of pine trees behind Alfred's family's home, stood a small shrine dedicated to Our Lady of Lourdes.

Alfred parked the car among the trees and said, "I'll be right back," taking with him the flowers he had bought me for his graduation night. After spending a moment in the chapel, he came back to get me.

Looking very excited, ready to surprise me with the perfect ending to a glorious night, Albert opened the car door, reached for my hand, and led me toward the chapel. I stepped inside to see an altar supporting an elegant statue of Our Lady of Lourdes, outlined by a beautiful, gothic stained-glass window behind her. Bouquets of flowers surrounded Mary, and candles danced on all four walls. On a pew lay the flowers Alfred had gotten me that night. . . and next to the flowers there lay . . . a small box. My eyes fixated on the box and couldn't move. I recognized what it was immediately. Just days before, Alfred had taken my birthstone ring so that he could have something from me to hold onto, and he could have easily sized an engagement ring.

The two of us stood side by side facing Mary. Then Alfred turned to me and said, "This is the night I was waiting for. I've been wanting to ask you to marry me. We have talked about marriage, and wouldn't it be beautiful? This engagement can remain just between the two of us. No one needs to know. . . I'm leaving this Sunday, and you can carry this ring with you, not telling anyone, just like I'm carrying your ring."

Looking intently at me, Alfred could tell something was wrong. I looked and felt startled and aloof, so he began to cover his tracks, explaining why he'd chosen this night and the logic behind it: "Oh, I am sorry. I should have let you know, but since I'm leaving and didn't want to make it a family affair, just something between the two of us before God, I wanted to put this ring on your finger. . . something for you to hold onto during the time I'm not here. Well . . . I just wanted you to know that even though I am going away, I am yours forever."

With those perfect words, I looked back at him, and a cool darkness fell over my heart.

"Are you all right?" he asked. "I thought this was where we were in the relationship. Are you okay with this?"

I responded simply, "I don't understand myself." The more he talked, the more I felt something come between us, and I didn't know what it was. It had no name.

"What is it? What is happening?"

"I don't know. I don't know."

Crestfallen and bewildered, he asked, "Well, where do we go from here? You know I'm leaving."

I couldn't speak or answer any of his questions. Here was the man of my dreams asking me for his hand in marriage. We had talked marriage, children, a life together, and never did I doubt doing any of this with him. I wanted to be with him, and I would marry him and no one else. I had wanted this all my life, and now, within minutes, my heart had grown stone cold.

Finally, we packed up in a daze. He closed the box, put it in his pocket, blew out the candles, and packed up the flowers. He was devastated, and so was I, and no explanation reached my conscious mind, which made everything even worse.

"Do you have anything else to say besides 'I don't know'?" he blurted out. "Is there anybody else? Are you not sure? But you sounded sure." And that was true. Up until just one hour earlier, I had been sure. We drove home in an uncomfortable, bitter silence, and every so often, he just shook his head.

The end of the night went from bad to worse. Usually we stood by my door and kissed goodbye, holding each other. But that night I just stood there with my arms hanging down, like a sack of potatoes. He couldn't believe what was happening. "I'll come back on Sunday to say, 'Goodbye,' and please tell me what's going on. I can't imagine leaving like this."

So without a kiss, an embrace, or an explanation, he slowly turned around and walked to the car; and I walked in the door and into the most horrible three days of my life.

# 4) Locked in darkness

L ocked inside myself, in utter darkness, I searched in vain for why I was feeling this way. Wasn't I in love with the most wonderful man in Germany just a couple days ago? Everyone thought this man was extraordinary, the best of the best, and so did I.

My opinion of Alfred hadn't changed whatsoever, but my feelings for him had vanished into thin air. They were gone, completely. I felt like ice. Thinking about him day and night and talking to him constantly in my mind, I tried to find the words to explain what had happened, but I couldn't grasp them. Whatever I came up with didn't make sense. . . The whole experience didn't make sense. Never before had I felt this way, even for a brief moment.

Time felt like forever until I could see him again, and then on Sunday, when I heard his motorbike pull up the front drive, a cool darkness washed over me, and again all feeling died. My mom called upstairs and said, "Come down, honey."

I couldn't bring myself to tell my family or anyone what was going on. My parents liked Alfred; my sisters liked Alfred; even my protective brothers liked Alfred. He was already part of my family, and I belonged to his.

When Alfred stood in the front door, he looked like a ghost. "Would you like to take a walk?" he asked.

"Yes," I responded.

We walked outside behind my home into a meadow sprinkled with summer wild flowers. Acres of grass and trees dovetailed into rolling hills, extending to the River Main. Germany is stunning in May, but my eyes couldn't see any of its beauty. Alfred planted himself in front of me and looking directly in my eyes, said, "You must tell me what has happened. I need to know. I haven't been able to sleep. Please tell me what's going on."

Everything I did and felt was unfair to him, but I had nothing to say. I went dumb. Again, all I could muster was, "I don't know. I don't know," with a cold, distant look.

"That is not an answer," he responded. "We've known each other for four years and have been dating for two. You can't just say, 'I don't know.' You have to have a reason."

I shook my head and started to cry. I felt so worn out. "I really do not know. And I would love to say yes to you, but I cannot."

Then he said, "What is this? Is there anybody else in this whole wide world, or something else in this world that is stopping you?"

"I don't know of anything," I said in anguish. "There is nobody else . . . and nothing else. But I cannot give you my heart. I know you would want me to give it to you, and that is why this is so horrible, because I want to give you my heart. And if I say yes now, you wouldn't want that either. You would want my whole heart, not just a yes from my mouth."

Shaking his head, he said, "No, if you don't mean it, don't say it." Slumping to the ground in despair, he fell silent. Then with a hollow voice, he asked, "Where do we go from here?"

Exhausted from crying, I whispered, "I don't know."

Alfred's voice began to crack. "What do we do? Is it finished? Is this the end?"

"All I know is I cannot say yes. I cannot say anything. I will need some time. That means we don't write, we don't call, and we let each other be."

"I guess so. But if you would have cut me limb by limb, you couldn't have hurt me more than you did."

I already felt horrible, and his words took me to the darkest place I had ever been in my life. "I am so sorry," I cried. "I am so sorry."

When he left, I clutched myself in pain, believing I had to get my head examined.

I couldn't tell anyone what was happening. No one would understand, especially when I didn't even know myself. I moved into my mother's old room in my grandmother's house in order to be near summer school, but I studied poorly. Unable to concentrate or sleep, I spent half of my nights trying to figure out what was wrong with me.

Grasping for an escape or an answer, I started to read books, not my study books—anything but, in order to keep my thoughts off myself. I didn't sleep well for days. My mind played out my life like a film strip cut short by an abrupt end that made no sense. I felt as though I had been watching an entertaining movie, and then a malfunction in the projector suddenly left the theater quiet and pitch black. Everyone had vacated the premises, but I couldn't leave, so I had to sit paralyzed and alone, unable to rewind or play the film forward.

One evening, anticipating another sleepless night, I climbed into my grandmother's attic where I noticed a small library of religious books. When I asked my grandmother where they came from, she said that a few years back, she had hosted a young woman who had died there from tuberculosis. The woman had a brother in the seminary, whose books she stored, and when she passed, nobody claimed them.

The first books I brought down were philosophy books—too dry and hard to read. Then I picked up and read some of the lives of the saints. At least they offered stories I could follow, which helped my mind to focus better. Then I came across a book on the desert fathers.

A desert father named Anthony had found the woman of his dreams, I read. Everything about this woman was right for him, but he never married her and didn't know why not. One day she confronted him, "I am getting older and older, and why are you not making up your mind?" But he couldn't. Something held him back, and he lost the girl.

In the story, Anthony came to realize that he was in love with love more than he was in love with her. Bells suddenly rang in my mind, clanging with truth. I, too, was in love with love! I was more enamored with the idea of romantic love than I was with Alfred himself!

All of my life, my parents had played out the great love story before my eyes, and seeking a relationship like theirs had become life's meaning and purpose for me. I wanted romance. I wanted love. But the object of my affection was true Love!

If you would have heard me talk about marriage to the Catholic youth, you would have been convinced that holy matrimony was heaven on earth. I could make everyone believe this because of the feelings that overcame me when I looked at my parents.

Lying on my back in bed, I continued to read: "Wondering over his own reluctance to get married, Anthony turned to the Lord and said, 'I couldn't give her my heart. Is it You who wants my heart?'"

Upon reading those words, I closed the book over my heart and said, "Lord, if it is You Who wants my heart, then all of this would make sense." And then, for the first time in weeks, I drifted off to sleep. By that time, the people in my neighborhood had been gossiping with each other over what I could possibly be doing throughout the night because my room light was always on: "Is she studying that late? Nobody can study that many hours." But from that night forward, I gave them nothing to talk about.

For the rest of the summer, before fading into sleep at night, I asked God, "Lord, is it You Who wants my heart?" And slowly, nearly imperceptibly, into my complete darkness, there emerged a tiny, grey light that grew a little brighter and a little bigger each day I said that prayer.

My grandmother prayed the Rosary every night and always invited me to join her, but I never stayed downstairs to pray and excused myself to study. One night, I declined her offer again but went upstairs to my room and promptly took my mother's statue of Mary, which stood humbly in the corner of the room, and put her proudly by my feet, like a nightstand. Something made me turn to her for the first time in my life. Never before had I prayed a Rosary by myself, but as I lay down for the night, I began saying "Hail Mary's" half-aloud, sometimes adding, "Mary, if it's your Son who wants my heart, I want to know. I am willing and ready to give it over to Him." Each "Hail Mary" sent soothing waves of peace cascading through me, as I looked at her, and she looked back at me, seemingly real and present. My mind and body craved rest, and from that point on, I felt my mother in heaven lull me each night into a deep, peaceful sleep.

By the end of summer, it became clear to me that I wanted to give my heart to God. The prayer and the peace had given me my answer. One morning, as a sign of my commitment, I took a dried edelweiss, which Alfred had picked for me from the highest Alps, and mounted the flower onto a small marble rock. On it, I inscribed: "Like a flower on a mountain top, far away from the eyes of all, only for the glory of God, I want to live."

# 5) Not the nunny type

----------------------------------------

inally, I felt ready to speak to someone about my interior life, so I traveled to see my youth chaplain, Fr. Hafe, who knew both me and Alfred well.

My news astonished him. "You want to be a nun?" he asked incredulously. "That doesn't sound right." Then he giggled, "So on Alfred's graduation night . . . that closed white collar you were wearing, unlike all the other girls . . . that was the beginning of your convent outfit! I should have known better. . ."

"No, no!" I said to him. I didn't know any nuns personally, nor did I admire any. "I just want to give my heart to God. That's all."

He shook his head in disbelief. "This is terrible. I can see that you are okay, but how is Alfred?"

"I never talked to him after the break up. I worry and think of him every day, but I don't know how he is. Meanwhile, I need your help. You see, I am not the nunny type. I don't want to join an order of sisters because I won't fit in. They're too devout. They whisper in soft, funny, little voices, and they walk around with their hands folded under their habits, staring at the ground."

My mind was running tricks trying to imagine myself as a Catholic sister. I couldn't stomach the thought of living in a house with a bunch of women. In my home growing up, I'd lived with four men—my dad and three brothers, and four women—my mother and three sisters, and I felt no need to narrow things down. Nobody ever thought, when they looked at my family, that I would grow up to be a nun because nothing about me as a young girl seemed pious. I was newfangled and mischievous, always gravitating instinctively toward the limelight and showing deference to no one.

With great sincerity, I said, "Maybe I should become a hermitess and pray alone on a mountain top."

Fr. Hafe laughed. "You would never be alone on top of the mountain. Very soon the mountain would be swarming with men."

So he was not very encouraging. At this point, I felt my words were digging into a dry well. Shoveling one last try, I said, "Well, you could help by pointing out where I could start. I can give you a list of lots of addresses of monasteries. There are many different kinds. . ."

He looked at me and repeated, "You don't fit. You don't fit them. Of all the nuns I know, you just don't fit."

A week and a half later, Alfred showed up in Fr. Hafe's office. He had spent much of his time over the summer getting counseling from his camp's chaplain priest and hadn't been much of a camp counselor himself. The chaplain, wanting some sleep, encouraged him to return home to talk with me and the youth chaplain in order to find some answers. Alfred sat in front of Fr. Hafe, in the same seat I'd occupied a couple weeks earlier, and began to share his story to the disbelieving priest.

One night in camp, after weeks of grief and turmoil, Alfred had climbed up a moonlit mountain and sat down in a clearing overlooking the valley. Whether he fell asleep or not, he doesn't know. His whole being entered into brief trance, and in that short time, he had a clear vision of the Lord Jesus appearing before him and saying to him, "Remember your first love. You wanted to give your life to me as a priest, and you only left the seminary because your father removed you. Then you fell in love with Maria and forgot about your first love. Now you are free to go back to the One you loved first."

When he woke up, all made sense. He had always longed to go back to the seminary and to his life of prayer there after his father had taken him away. As soon as summer camp was over, Alfred mounted his motorbike and said to himself, "You are twenty-five. You'd better get back into the seminary, before it's too late."

Fr. Hafe shook his head. "I can't believe it. This is unreal. You should talk to Maria. I think she would want to see you."

"I wrote her everything in a letter. Thirteen double-sided pages."

I received that letter at my parents' house, the end of that summer. Tearing it open with anxious anticipation, nervously wondering what he would say on so many pages, I began to read. When I came to the end, I re-read it, again and again, crying from relief. With words and meaning so full and rich, it set my heart free. I couldn't believe the plan of God. Everything had to happen the way it did. I would never have considered religious life if the darkness hadn't come over me, and Alfred would never have entered the seminary if I had given my yes that night in his father's chapel. Of our own free will, we wouldn't have created the space to make such drastic decisions, sending our lives in completely different directions. How well God knew our souls! All had always been totally clear to Him, yet completely mysterious to us.

After three straight days of poring over Alfred's letter, now wrinkled and smudged from my grasp and my tears,

Alfred showed up at my doorstep unannounced. With the youth chaplain's recommendation, he had driven his motorbike to my parents' home, where I was now living because summer school was over.

"Hello, may I see Maria?" he said to my family, who greeted him warmly at the door.

As I came down the stairs to meet him, our eyes met with expectation: he knowing I'd received the letter, and I wondering if the chaplain had told him anything about me.

Side by side, we left my parents' house and walked out into the fields behind my family home. It was now July. The first tall grasses had been cut down by the farmers to make hay, supplanted by the new grass of summer, made plentiful by the sprinkled seeds from the May harvest. Shades of lush and bright green, blanketed the fields and draped the hills.

Over two months had passed since Alfred and I stood in those fields, facing each other, with desperate hearts, immune to the natural beauty surrounding us. Now, as we looked at one another, the warmth of the air, the smell of fresh grass, and the bright hews of the rolling landscape embraced our senses.

Taking a deep breath, I began, "I must tell you something," and I poured out my story—my anguish over the way I parted from him, my utter darkness and doubts over my own sanity . . . then the small spark of light . . . and finally the call from God. Whereas before, I had felt muted, unable to share a word or an ounce of understanding, now I couldn't stop speaking. Finally, my story ran into the present moment, and I said, "Now I want to give my life to God, and I do not know how."

Alfred looked elated. "I cannot believe it! I cannot believe it!" he exclaimed. I marveled at his exuberant joy, realizing he was hearing my story for the first time. His happiness over learning of my calling surpassed even my joy upon discovering his. The struggle within him hadn't been against returning to seminary—God's call for him to the priesthood was clear and what his heart desired. But Alfred still had not let go of me. By no means could he imagine, or did he want to see me in the arms of another man. His greatest sacrifice was to set me free.

Now we were free for God, free to journey our separate ways without fear or angst, but that didn't take away the attraction between us. We knew we would have to stay apart by choice. In fact, our attraction for one another grew even stronger. Like little kids, we danced around, out in the fields, to a heavenly, yet bittersweet song. Alfred felt so free again that he began singing my name, as he had always done, when in good spirits. "You are more romantic than all the romantics in Germany put together," I teased him.

Alfred knew my heart. He knew there was more to me than my outgoing personality, so my calling made sense to him— or he wanted it to make sense. Being older and more experienced than I, he also knew more about convents in Germany. If you talked to me about men and marriage, I could spout something convincing. Ask me about convents, and I could offer nothing.

Alfred gave me the addresses of cloistered and semi-cloistered convents to write to and to visit, and we agreed we wouldn't tell anyone what we were up to. "No one must know we've even broken up," we told one another. Being popular in the eyes of the diocese, and proud, neither of us wanted people to think that the other had ended the relationship, thus driving us towards religious life. So we decided that rather than spread our wings to show them off to others, we'd let our beautiful feathers be discovered naturally over time.

IN LOVE WITH TRUE LOVE

# 6) Looking out for me

------------------------------------------------

That entire fall, I looked at various religious communities, coercing other boys from the Catholic youth group to go with me, in case my family discovered my whereabouts. But none of the congregations appealed to me. Finally, I had to tell my parents that I had split with Alfred and wanted to become a nun . . . or something. They had to know, since I was no longer going to leave for college to the city I loved most, Freiburg, and they wouldn't understand this change of plans. When my parents heard my big news, they chuckled. "You're not the type," my mom quipped, and my father gasped, "No way. I can't imagine you out there riding, cycling, and partying in a convent. Just because you broke things off with Alfred, don't worry . . . Please don't act on anything right now, you will be fine. I won't give you any money for the convent until you have thought about this for a long time." But I wanted to enter a convent—or whatever it was—right away.

When September came, I had to do something. A brand-new Catholic boarding school had just opened, so I thought I'd enroll there, at least for one semester, to get away and think. I had no idea what I was doing. By January of 1957, I had entered the school and soon found out that the diocese had stuffed it with nuns. I couldn't believe my eyes. Nuns whom I could watch in secret. Nuns unaware of what I was up to were living and praying, day in and day out, right in front of me.

These Dominican sisters of Oakford, based primarily in South Africa, lived as active contemplatives and missionaries. Their convent was the world. Vesting a blue and white habit with a veil and knee-length skirt, they fully lived out the commands of the Gospel and took a strict vow of poverty, begging for their food two times a year. Naturally attracting the young, their superior was age thirty-two and the rest in their twenties. But what spoke most to me was their spirit. While open and fun, full of laughter and very human, they also showed a serious and contemplative side. Sitting in the church for hours of prayer, they communed with God in silence or through the divine office, singing in angelic tones. I liked them. And although I wasn't known as a particularly pious student, they liked me, too.

The longer I lived there, the more I identified with the sisters, and finally at Easter, I approached the school chaplain and told him what I had in mind. In 1956, at age twenty, I entered the novitiate and took my first step toward becoming a Catholic nun. That same year, Alfred re-entered the seminary. Among our friends and acquaintances from the Catholic youth group, gossip spread like fire.

Three years later, I took my final vows as a Dominican sister of Oakford. Shortly after that, Alfred took vows with the Benedictine order and was sent to Kenya, then Tanzania, where he lived the rest of his days as a great priest, monk, and missionary. When Alfred made his vows, he took the name Klaus of Flüe, because Klaus was the patron of the German Catholic youth in Germany where we had worked together. But there was another reason why Alfred, now Klaus, took that name. The name Klaus is short for Nicholas. When Klaus visited home, he always called himself Nicholas because it made him feel and sound closer to me. He loved to talk about it, confessing to the world, "I'm Nicholas, and she's Nicolina." Then with an ear-to-ear smile, he'd add, "Well, she didn't take my name, so I took hers!" Intertwining us even more, during my vows, the priest chaplain of the school happened to give me the name Nicolina, after the same St. Klaus of the Flüe to whom the Dominican School was dedicated.

Klaus was able to travel home to Germany every three years, and I, every five years, so he always tried to come when I was there. In 1959, when my order assigned me to live in California, Klaus still found a way to visit. His family had money so when his sister asked him what she could get him, he always answered, "A ticket to California."

Whenever Klaus came to visit me at the convent in California, he would pass through an assembly of women in habits, with a bright sparkle in his eye and a large bouquet of flowers in his hand, and then present them to me with great fanfare. The sisters always laughed because I looked so embarrassed. Free, joyful, and uninhibited in expressing himself—that was Klaus. Everybody in the convent loved him and felt happy about our relationship, which was beautiful and clean.

In 2006, when I had been a Dominican sister of Oakford for fifty-two years, and Klaus had just turned seventy, I received a short email from him: "Please pray for me. I have cancer, and they will operate on me tomorrow. I will let you know if I survive." Riddled with the disease, he was flown to a mission hospital in Germany.

Every day at 12 o'clock in California—9 p.m. in Germany, Klaus would call me, and we would talk and pray, sharing our hearts over the telephone. Before hanging up, I always said a

German prayer to Mary, asking her to accompany us into paradise. It was a prayer Klaus and I had said together in our youth, over forty-six years earlier.

Toward the end, Klaus couldn't speak, but I could hear his breathing. "Can you hear me?" I would ask, and his brother-in-law would speak into the phone, "He does; he's nodding." Each day in the hospital, when it came close to noon, Klaus would point to the clock, wanting the nurses to leave because it was time for us to be together. "Klaus," I told him, "make sure you let me know if you are in heaven, or where you are, after you die." And I reminded him often, "Please look after me."

When he could still speak, he gave me his promise. "In life or in death, I will always look after you."

Klaus died on a day that I couldn't get to the phone. Every day, for months, we had been in contact as he was dying, and then he was simply gone. I felt numb. A growing ache formed in my heart, followed by unexpected waves of crushing grief. If Klaus had been my husband, I couldn't have gotten more cards. Everyone we knew tried to console me and let me know they were thinking of me.

After his death, I prayed, "Klaus, look after me. Please watch after me," but I never sensed a response or a sign. Often, I wondered, "Where are you now? I believe you are in heaven, but where is this heaven? It feels so far away."

Then five months after Klaus passed, I had a dream, a crystal-clear vision, which I remember as though it happened minutes ago. Klaus's face appeared before me on my right, and traveled slowly sideways across my vision. Surrounded by a bright golden light, unlike any on earth, Klaus smiled and his eyes were upon me, as they always had been in life.

But one thing was different. On earth, Klaus had never

been a nervous man. When he held you in his gaze, he looked at you with direct, unflinching attention. But now his eyes had changed. They were no longer veiled with desire. They had seen something far more glorious than anything here on earth and expressed a profound contentment. As his face disappeared beyond the left side of my vision, I knew Klaus was utterly and perfectly fulfilled.

Since that dream, not a sign of sadness or loss has burdened my heart. I do not miss Klaus anymore. When I think of him, I simply feel love; and I know now, without a doubt, that in death, just as in life, Alfred is looking out for me.

# SISTER NICOLINA KOHLER

(named after St. Nicholas of Flüe, also known as Brother Klaus)

The fascinating story of Sr. Nicolina's illumination of conscience, during which she suddenly saw the state of her soul through the eyes of Jesus, can be found in the #1 best-selling book:

*The Warning: Testimonies and Prophecies of*
*the Illumination of Conscience.*

# Notes to the reader

---

## Amazon Reviews

If you were graced by this book, would you kindly post a short review of *In Love with True Love* on Amazon.com? Your support will make a difference in the lives and vocations of souls.

To leave a short review, go to Amazon.com and type in *In Love with True Love*. Click on the book and scroll down the page. Next to customer reviews, click on "Write a customer review." Thank you, in advance, for your kindness.

## Newsletter

Sign up for the Queen of Peace Media monthly newsletter to be informed of resources to help you navigate these tumultuous times and Find Your Way Home.

### www.QueenofPeaceMedia.com/newsletter

## Messages from Heaven

If you are interested in learning about what Our Lord and Our Lady are purportedly saying to the world for our times, see:

### www.CountdowntotheKingdom.com.

# Other books by the author

----------------------------------------

available through
QueenofPeaceMedia.com and Amazon.com
in Print, Ebook, and Audiobook formats

## Libros disponible en español

www.queenofpeacemedia.com/libreria-catolica

### EL AVISO

Testimonios y Profecías de la Iluminación de
Conciencia

### EL MANTO DE MARÍA

Una Consagración Mariana para Ayuda Celestial

### EL MANTO DE MARÍA

Diario de Oración para la Consagración

### TRANSFIGURADA

La Historia de Patricia Sandoval

### HOMBRES JUNTO A MARÍA

Así Vencieron Seis Hombres la Más Ardua
Batalla de Sus Vidas

# THE WARNING

## TESTIMONIES AND PROPHECIES OF
## THE ILLUMINATION OF CONSCIENCE
### with *IMPRIMATUR*

### *en español:*
# EL AVISO

**Endorsed by Bishop Gavin Ashenden, Msgr. Ralph J. Chieffo, Fr. John Struzzo, Mark Mallet, Fr. Berdardin Mugabo, and more…**

**Includes the fascinating story of Marino Restrepo, hailed as a St. Paul for our century**

(See www.queenofpeacemedia.com/the-warning for the book trailer)

*The Warning* has been an Amazon #1 best-seller, ever since its release. In the book are authentic accounts of saints and mystics of the Church who have spoken of a day when we will all see our souls in the light of truth, and fascinating stories of those who have already experienced it for themselves.

*"With His divine love, He will open the doors of hearts and illuminate all consciences. Every person will see himself in the burning fire of divine truth. It will be like a judgment in miniature."*
**—Our Lady to Fr. Stefano Gobbi of the Marian Movement of Priests**

47

# SHE WHO SHOWS THE WAY

## HEAVEN'S MESSAGES
## FOR OUR TURBULENT TIMES

"This book should be widely disseminated, all for God's glory and in honor of the Mother of God, for all of us and the holiness of Christ's disciples."
— Ramón C. Argüelles, STL, Archbishop-Emeritus

(See www.QueenofPeaceMedia.com and Amazon.com)

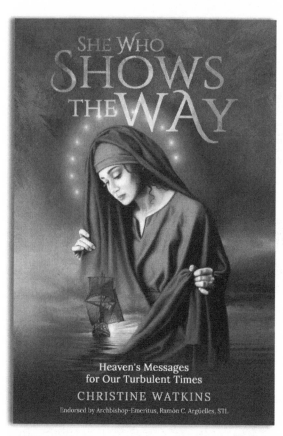

Our Mother knows when we most need her, and we need her now.

We are living in the end times, not the end of the world, but the end of an age. Those who wish to remain faithful to the Gospel are seeking heaven's guidance in order to weather and safely navigate the unparalleled storms ahead.

In this extraordinary and anointed book of messages from Mother Mary—and occasionally from Jesus—through inner-locutions to one of her most unlikely children, she has responded.

"A great turning point in the fate of your nation and its faith in God will soon be upon you, and I ask you all to pray and offer your sufferings for this cause. . ."
— Our Lady's message of August 4, 1993

# OF MEN AND MARY

## HOW SIX MEN WON THE GREATEST BATTLE OF THEIR LIVES

*"Of Men and Mary* is superb. The six life testimonies contained within it are miraculous, heroic, and truly inspiring."

— **Fr. Gary Thomas**
Pastor, exorcist, and subject of the book and movie, "The Rite."

### "Anointed!"
— **Fr. Donald Calloway, MIC**

(See <u>www.queenofpeacemedia.com/of-men-and-mary</u>
For the book trailer and to order)

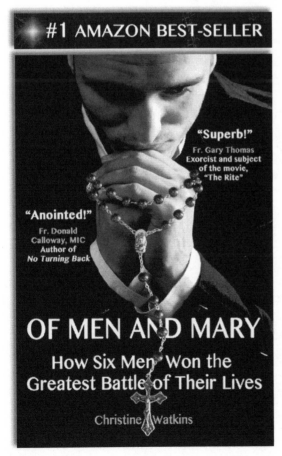

Turn these pages, and you will find yourself surprisingly inspired by a murderer locked up in prison, a drug-using football player who dreamed of the pros, and a selfish, womanizing daredevil who died and met God. You will root for a husband and father whose marriage was a battleground, a man searching desperately to belong, pulled by lust and illicit attractions, and an innocent lamb who lost, in a single moment, everyone he cared about most. And you will rejoice that their sins and their pasts were no obstacle for heaven.

# FULL OF GRACE

## MIRACULOUS STORIES OF HEALING AND CONVERSION THROUGH MARY'S INTERCESSION

"Christine Watkins's beautiful and touching collection of conversion stories are direct, honest, heart-rending, and miraculous."

**—Wayne Weible**
Author of *Medjugorje: The Message*

**(See www.queenofpeacemedia.com/full-of-grace**
**for the book trailer and to order)**

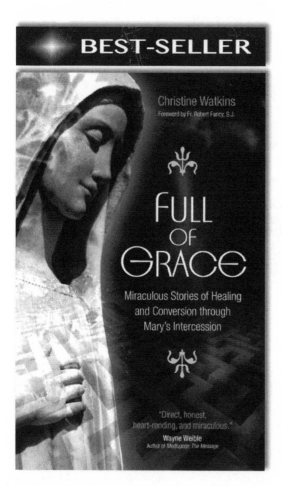

In this riveting book, Christine Watkins tells her dramatic story of miraculous healing and conversion to Catholicism, along with the stories of five others: a homeless drug addict, an altar boy trapped by cocaine, a stripper, a lonely youth, and a modern-day hero. Following each story is a message that Mary has given to the world.

And for those eager to probe the deeper, reflective waters of discipleship—either alone or within a prayer group—a Scripture passage, prayerful reflection questions, and a spiritual exercise at the end of each chapter offer an opportunity to enliven our faith.

# TRANSFIGURED

## PATRICIA SANDOVAL'S STORY

Endorsed by
**Archbishop Salvatore Cordileone & Bishop Michael C. Barber, SJ,
And Fr. Donald Calloway, MIC**

**Disponible También en Español: TRANSFIGURADA
avalado por EMMANUEL**

(See <u>www.queenofpeacemedia.com/transfigured</u>
for the book trailer, the companion DVD, and to order)

"Are you ready to read one of the most powerful conversion stories ever written? Seriously, are you? It's a bold and shocking claim, I admit. But the story you are about to have the pleasure of reading is so intense and brutally candid that I wouldn't be surprised if it brings you to tears multiple times and opens the door to an experience of mercy and healing. This story is made for the big screen, and I pray it makes it there someday. It's that incredible. . . What you are about to read is as raw, real, and riveting as a story can get. I couldn't put this book down!"

**—Fr. Donald Calloway, MIC**
Author of
*Consecration to St. Joseph*
and *No Turning Back*

51

# MARY'S MANTLE CONSECRATION

## A SPIRITUAL RETREAT FOR HEAVEN'S HELP

Disponible también en español—*El Manto de María: Una Consagración Mariana para Ayuda Celestial*

Endorsed by **Archbishop Salvatore Cordileone** and **Bishop Myron J. Cotta**

(See www.MarysMantleConsecration.com to see a video of amazing testimonies and to order)

"I am grateful to Christine Watkins for making this disarmingly simple practice, which first grew in the fertile soil of Mexican piety, available to the English-speaking world."
—**Archbishop Salvatore Cordileone**

"Now more than ever, we need a miracle. Christine Watkins leads us through a 46-day self-guided retreat that focuses on daily praying of the Rosary, a Little fasting, and meditating on various virtues and the seven gifts of the Holy Spirit, leading to a transformation in our lives and in the people on the journey with us!"
—**Fr. Sean O. Sheridan, TOR**
Former President, Franciscan University of Steubenville

# MARY'S MANTLE
# CONSECRATION

## PRAYER JOURNAL
**to accompany the consecration book**

**Disponible también en español—**
*El Manto de Maria: Diario de Oración para la Consagración*

## PREPARE FOR AN OUTPOURING
## OF GRACE UPON YOUR LIFE

**(See www.MarysMantleConsecration.com
to see a video of amazing testimonies and to order)**

St. Pope John Paul II said that his consecration to Mary was "a decisive turning point in my life." It can be the same for you.

This *Prayer Journal* with daily Scriptures, saint quotes, questions for reflection and space for journaling is a companion book to the popular *Mary's Mantle Consecration*, a self-guided retreat that has resulted in miracles in the lives and hearts of those who have applied themselves to it. This prayer journal will take you even deeper into your soul and into God's transforming grace.

# WINNING THE BATTLE FOR YOUR SOUL

## JESUS' TEACHINGS THROUGH MARINO RESTREPO, A ST. PAUL FOR OUR CENTURY

Endorsed by Archbishop-Emeritus, Ramón C. Argüelles
"This book is an authentic jewel of God!"
—Internationally renowned author, María Vallejo-Nájera
(See <u>The Warning: Testimonies and Prophecies of the Illumination of Conscience</u> to read Marino's testimony)

Marino Restrepo was a sinful man kidnapped for ransom by Colombian terrorists and dragged into the heart of the Amazon jungle. In the span of just one night, the Lord gave him an illumination of his conscience followed by an extraordinary infusion of divine knowledge. Today, Marino is hailed as one of the greatest evangelizers of our time.

In addition to giving talks around the world, Marino is the founder of the Church-approved aposto- late, Pilgrims of Love.

This little book contains some of the most extraordinary teachings that Jesus has given to the world through Marino Restrepo, teachings that will profoundly alter and inform the way you see your ancestry, your past, your purpose, your future, and your very salvation.

# MARIE-JULIE JAHENNY

## PROPHECIES AND PROTECTION
## FOR THE END TIMES

**(See www.QueenofPeaceMedia.com. Soon on Amazon.com)**

Marie-Julie Jahenny (1850-1941) is one of the most extraordinary mystics in the history of the Church. This humble peasant from devout parents in Britanny, France, received numerous visitations from heaven and lived with multiple wounds of the stigmata for most of her long life.

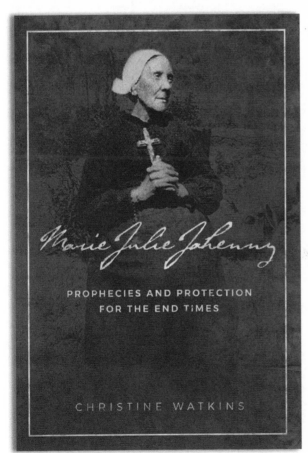

Jahenny's selfless spirit endures as a gift to the Church, for she received knowledge of what lies on the horizon of our current era.

Jahenny was supported by her local bishop, Msgr. Fournier of Nantes, who said of her, "I see nothing but good."

In addition to Jahenny's special mission from the Lord to spread the love of the Cross, she was called to prepare the world for the coming chastisements, which precede and prepare the world for the glorious renewal of Christendom in the promised era of peace.

Through Marie-Julie, the Lord has given help, remedies, and protection for the times we now live in, and those soon to come. As Christ said to her on several occasions, "I want My people to be warned."

# PURPLE SCAPULAR

## OF BLESSING AND PROTECTION FOR THE END TIMES

**Jesus and Mary have given this scapular to the world for our times!**

Go to **www.queenofpeacemedia.com/product/purple-scapular-of-blessing-and-protection** to read about all of the incredible promises given to those who wear it in faith.

**Our Lady's words to the mystic, stigmatist, and victim soul, Marie-Julie Jahenny:** "My children, all souls, all people who possesses this scapular will see their family protected. Their home will also be protected, **foremost from fires**. . . for a long time my Son and I have had the desire to make known this scapular of benediction…

This first apparition of this scapular will be a new protection for the times of the chastisements, of the calamities, and the famines. All those who are clothed (with it) shall pass under the storms, the tempests, and the darkness. They will have light as if it were plain day. Such is the power of this unknown scapular…"

# THE FLAME OF LOVE

## THE SPIRITUAL DIARY
## OF ELIZABETH KINDELMANN

(See [www.QueenofPeaceMedia.com/flame-love-love-book-bundle](http://www.QueenofPeaceMedia.com/flame-love-love-book-bundle))

Extraordinary graces of literally blinding Satan, and reaching heaven quickly are attached to the spiritual practices and promises in this spiritual classic. On August 2, 1962, Our Lady said these remarkable words to mystic and victim soul, Elizabeth Kindelmann:

**"Since the Word became Flesh, I have never given such a great movement as the Flame of Love that comes to you now. Until now, there has been nothing that so blinds Satan."**

# THE FLAME OF LOVE

In this special talk, Christine Watkins introduces the Flame of Love of the Immaculate Heart of Mary.

This worldwide movement in the Catholic Church is making true disciples of Jesus Christ in our turbulent times and preparing souls for the Triumph of Our Lady's Heart and the New Pentecost.

See www.ChristineWatkins.com.
Email cwatkins@queenofpeacemedia.com.

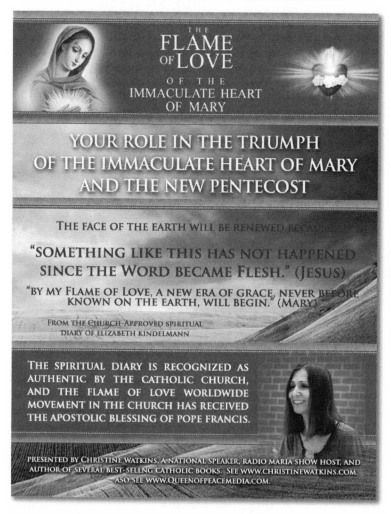

Made in the USA
Columbia, SC
13 February 2021